How to Use This Book

This reading and book review journal is the perfect way to keep track of your reading habits. The pages include space to record your favorite books, write reviews, reading challenges upcoming releases and trackers.

Books to read: this is where you can keep your to-be-read list. Includes space to jot down the book title, author and genre.

Reading log: space to track your weekly reading. Tick off the days that you read each week and write down the book, pages read and a few initial thoughts.

Book reviews: space to record details and thoughts on your books, including star ratings.

This Reading Journal Belongs To:

....

Test out your pens and markers on this page!

Books To Read

☐	BOOK TITLE	AUTHOR	GENRE
☐			
☐			
☐			
☐			
☐			
☐			
☐			
☐			
☐			
☐			
☐			
☐			

Books To Read

☐	BOOK TITLE	AUTHOR	GENRE
☐			
☐			
☐			
☐			
☐			
☐			
☐			
☐			
☐			
☐			
☐			
☐			

Books To Read

	BOOK TITLE	AUTHOR	GENRE
☐			
☐			
☐			
☐			
☐			
☐			
☐			
☐			
☐			
☐			
☐			
☐			

Books To Read

☐	BOOK TITLE	AUTHOR	GENRE
☐			
☐			
☐			
☐			
☐			
☐			
☐			
☐			
☐			
☐			
☐			
☐			

Book Reviews

Book Review

- Author:
- Book Title:
- Genre:
- Page Length:
- Year Published:
- Recommended: Y/N

Start Date:
Finish Date:

☆☆☆☆☆

Summary:

Memorable Quotes:

Book Review

Author:
Book Title:
Genre:
Page Length:
Year Published:
Recommended: Y/N

Start Date:
Finish Date:

☆☆☆☆☆

Summary:

Memorable Quotes:

Book Review

Author:

Book Title:

Genre:

Page Length:

Year Published:

Recommended: Y/N

Start Date:

Finish Date:

☆☆☆☆☆

Summary:

Memorable Quotes:

Book Review

Author:
Book Title:
Genre:
Page Length:
Year Published:
Recommended: Y/N

Start Date:
Finish Date:

☆ ☆ ☆ ☆ ☆

Summary:

Memorable Quotes:

Book Review

Author:

Book Title:

Genre:

Page Length:

Year Published:

Recommended: Y/N

Start Date:

Finish Date:

☆☆☆☆☆

Summary:

Memorable Quotes:

Book Review

Author:

Book Title:

Genre:

Page Length:

Year Published:

Recommended: Y/N

Start Date:

Finish Date:

☆☆☆☆☆

Summary:

Memorable Quotes:

Book Review

- Author:
- Book Title:
- Genre:
- Page Length:
- Year Published:
- Recommended: Y/N

Start Date:
Finish Date:

☆☆☆☆☆

Summary:

Memorable Quotes:

Book Review

Author:
Book Title:
Genre:
Page Length:
Year Published:
Recommended: Y/N

Start Date:
Finish Date:

☆☆☆☆☆

Summary:

Memorable Quotes:

Book Review

Author:

Book Title:

Genre:

Page Length:

Year Published:

Recommended: Y/N

Start Date:

Finish Date:

☆☆☆☆☆

Summary:

Memorable Quotes:

Book Review

Author:

Book Title:

Genre:

Page Length:

Year Published:

Recommended: Y/N

Start Date:

Finish Date:

☆ ☆ ☆ ☆ ☆

Summary:

Memorable Quotes:

Book Review

Author:

Book Title:

Genre:

Page Length:

Year Published:

Recommended: Y/N

Start Date:

Finish Date:

☆☆☆☆☆

Summary:

Memorable Quotes:

Book Review

Author:

Book Title:

Genre:

Page Length:

Year Published:

Recommended: Y/N

Start Date:

Finish Date:

☆☆☆☆☆

Summary:

Memorable Quotes:

Book Review

Author:

Book Title:

Genre:

Page Length:

Year Published:

Recommended: Y/N

Start Date:

Finish Date:

☆☆☆☆☆

Summary:

Memorable Quotes:

Book Review

Author:

Book Title:

Genre:

Page Length:

Year Published:

Recommended: Y/N

Start Date:

Finish Date:

☆☆☆☆☆

Summary:

Memorable Quotes:

Book Review

Author:
Book Title:
Genre:
Page Length:
Year Published:
Recommended: Y/N

Start Date:
Finish Date:

☆☆☆☆☆

Summary:

Memorable Quotes:

Book Review

Author:

Book Title:

Genre:

Page Length:

Year Published:

Recommended: Y/N

Start Date:

Finish Date:

☆☆☆☆☆

Summary:

Memorable Quotes:

Book Review

Author:

Book Title:

Genre:

Page Length:

Year Published:

Recommended: Y/N

Start Date:

Finish Date:

☆☆☆☆☆

Summary:

Memorable Quotes:

Book Review

Author:

Book Title:

Genre:

Page Length:

Year Published:

Recommended: Y/N

Start Date:

Finish Date:

Summary:

Memorable Quotes:

Book Review

Author:
Book Title:
Genre:
Page Length:
Year Published:
Recommended: Y/N

Start Date:
Finish Date:

☆☆☆☆☆

Summary:

Memorable Quotes:

Book Review

Author:

Book Title:

Genre:

Page Length:

Year Published:

Recommended: Y/N

Start Date:

Finish Date:

☆☆☆☆☆

Summary:

Memorable Quotes:

Reading Log

Reading Log

Year: S M T W T F S

Date	Author	Title	Pages

Reading Log

Year: _____   S M T W T F S

Date	Author	Title	Pages

Reading Log

Year: S   M   T   W   T   F   S

Date	Author	Title	Pages

Reading Log

Year: S M T W T F S

Date	Author	Title	Pages

Reading Log

Year: S   M   T   W   T   F   S

Date	Author	Title	Pages

Reading Log

Year: S M T W T F S

Date   Author   Title   Pages

Reading Log

Year: S M T W T F S

Date	Author	Title	Pages

Reading Log

Year: 　　　　　　　　S　M　T　W　T　F　S

Date	Author	Title	Pages

Reading Log

Year: S   M   T   W   T   F   S

Date	Author	Title	Pages

Reading Log

Year: S M T W T F S

Date	Author	Title	Pages

Reading Log

Year: S M T W T F S

Date   Author   Title   Pages

Reading Log

Year: ⠀⠀⠀⠀⠀⠀⠀⠀⠀⠀⠀ S ⠀ M ⠀ T ⠀ W ⠀ T ⠀ F ⠀ S

Date	Author	Title	Pages

Top Quotes

Date: S M T W T F S

Book Title: **Quotes:**

Author:

Book Title: **Quotes:**

Author:

Book Title: **Quotes:**

Author:

Top Quotes

Date: S M T W T F S

Book Title:

Author:

Quotes:

Book Title:

Author:

Quotes:

Book Title:

Author:

Quotes:

Top Quotes

Date: S   M   T   W   T   F   S

Book Title: **Quotes:**

Author:

Book Title: **Quotes:**

Author:

Book Title: **Quotes:**

Author:

My Reading Notes

Reading Notes

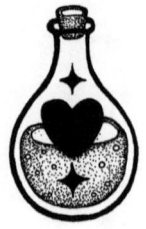

Date: S M T W T F S

My Notes

Reading Notes

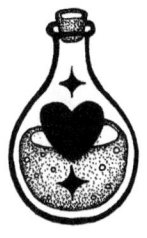

Date: S   M   T   W   T   F   S

My Notes

Reading Notes

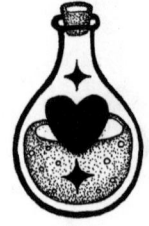

Date: S M T W T F S

My Notes

Reading Notes

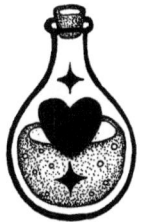

Date: S   M   T   W   T   F   S

My Notes

Reading Notes

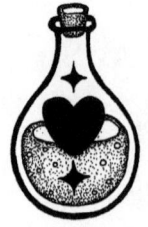

Date: S   M   T   W   T   F   S

My Notes

Reading Notes

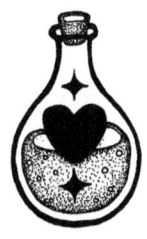

Date: S M T W T F S

My Notes

Reading Notes

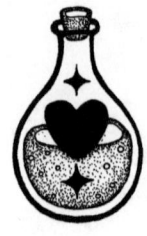

Date: S   M   T   W   T   F   S

My Notes

Reading Notes

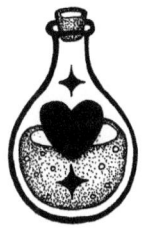

Date: S M T W T F S

My Notes

Reading Notes

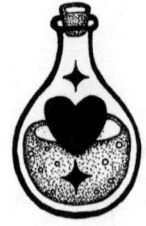

Date:　　　　　　　　　　　　　S M T W T F S

My Notes

Reading Notes

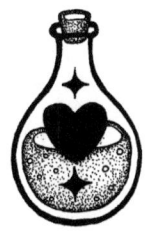

Date: S M T W T F S

My Notes

Reading Notes

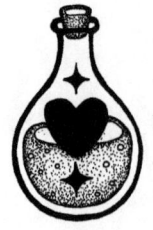

Date: S M T W T F S

My Notes

Reading Reflections

Reading REFLECTION

Date: _____

How I feel about this book:

😞 😐 🙂 😊 😁

The main reason for this is:
_____
_____
_____
_____

My favorite part was:
_____
_____
_____
_____
_____

I did not like:
_____
_____
_____
_____
_____

A quote I liked is:
_____
_____
_____

Reading REFLECTION

Date: _____

How I feel about this book:

☹ 😕 😐 🙂 😃

The main reason for this is:

_____
_____
_____

My favorite part was:

_____
_____
_____
_____
_____

I did not like:

_____
_____
_____
_____
_____

A quote I liked is:

_____
_____

Reading REFLECTION

Date: _____

How I feel about this book:

☹ 😐 🙂 😊 😃

The main reason for this is:

_____
_____
_____
_____

My favorite part was:

_____
_____
_____
_____
_____

I did not like:

_____
_____
_____
_____
_____

A quote I liked is:

_____
_____
_____

Reading REFLECTION

Date: _____

How I feel about this book:

☹️ 😐 🙂 😊 😃

The main reason for this is:

_____
_____
_____
_____

My favorite part was:

_____
_____
_____
_____
_____

I did not like:

_____
_____
_____
_____
_____

A quote I liked is:

_____
_____
_____

Reading REFLECTION

Date: _____

How I feel about this book:

☹ 😕 😐 🙂 😃

The main reason for this is:

_____
_____
_____
_____

My favorite part was:

_____
_____
_____
_____
_____

I did not like:

_____
_____
_____
_____
_____

A quote I liked is:

_____
_____

Reading REFLECTION

Date: _____

How I feel about this book:

☹️ 😕 😐 🙂 😀

The main reason for this is:

_____
_____
_____
_____

My favorite part was:

_____
_____
_____
_____
_____

I did not like:

_____
_____
_____
_____
_____

A quote I liked is:

_____
_____
_____

Reading REFLECTION

Date: _____

How I feel about this book:

☹ 😐 🙂 😊 😃

The main reason for this is:

_____
_____
_____
_____

My favorite part was:

_____
_____
_____
_____
_____

I did not like:

_____
_____
_____
_____
_____

A quote I liked is:

_____
_____

Reading REFLECTION

Date: _____

How I feel about this book:

😞 😐 😑 🙂 😃

The main reason for this is:

_____
_____
_____
_____

My favorite part was:

_____
_____
_____
_____
_____

I did not like:

_____
_____
_____
_____
_____

A quote I liked is:

_____
_____
_____

My Reading Notes

Reading Notes

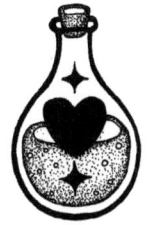

Date: S   M   T   W   T   F   S

My Notes

Reading Notes

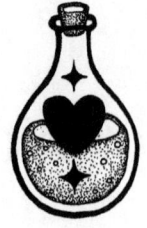

Date: S M T W T F S

My Notes

Reading Notes

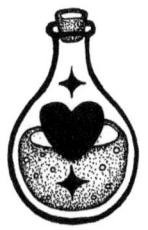

Date: S M T W T F S

My Notes

Reading Notes

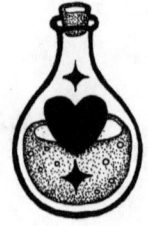

Date: S   M   T   W   T   F   S

My Notes

Reading Notes

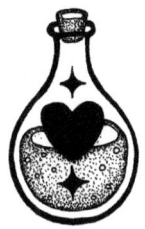

Date: S M T W T F S

My Notes

Reading Notes

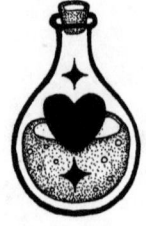

Date:　　　　　　　　　　　　S　M　T　W　T　F　S

My Notes

Reading Notes

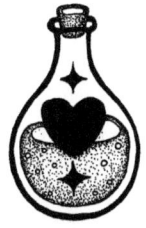

Date: S   M   T   W   T   F   S

My Notes

Reading Notes

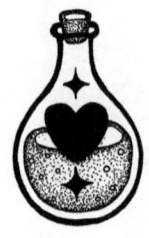

Date: S M T W T F S

My Notes

Reading Notes

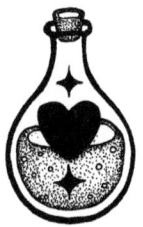

Date: S M T W T F S

My Notes

Reading Notes

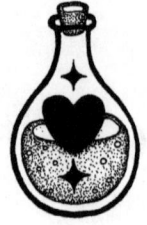

Date: S M T W T F S

My Notes

Reading Notes

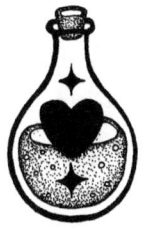

Date: S M T W T F S

My Notes

Book Notes

Book Notes

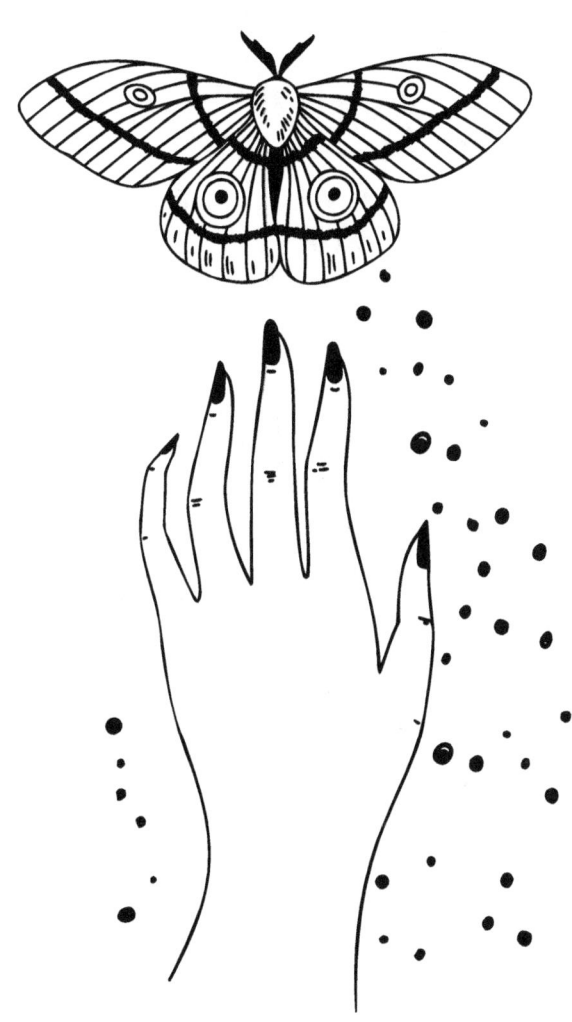

Colour me!

Colour me!

Book Bingo

A local author	Published this year	The first in a series	Book with an ocean on the cover	By a woman of color
Written by an immigrant	A Jane Austen Novel	A short story	Fairytale retelling	LGBTQIA+ author
Female main character	A book about a library or bookstore	FREE SPACE	Made into a movie	Science-Fiction
More than 350 pages	Book that has been banned in the past	A novella	Book set in China	Coming-of-age
About an animal	By a new author	A book you have never heard about before	Two female characters	Unreliable narrator

www.ingramcontent.com/pod-product-compliance
Lightning Source LLC
Chambersburg PA
CBHW061340040426
42444CB00011B/3006